Devils Tower

Tamara L. Britton
ABDO Publishing Company

visit us at
www.abdopub.com

Published by ABDO Publishing Company, 4940 Viking Drive, Edina, Minnesota 55435.
Copyright © 2005 by Abdo Consulting Group, Inc. International copyrights reserved in
all countries. No part of this book may be reproduced in any form without written
permission from the publisher. The Checkerboard Library™ is a trademark and logo of
ABDO Publishing Company.

Printed in the United States.

Cover Photo: Corbis
Interior Photos: Corbis pp. 1, 5, 6-7, 11, 13, 15, 26, 27, 28, 29, 31; Getty Images pp. 4,
    12, 17, 19, 25; Library of Congress pp. 19, 21; National Park Service p. 23

Series Coordinator: Heidi M. Dahmes
Editors: Heidi M. Dahmes, Stephanie Hedlund
Art Direction & Maps: Neil Klinepier

Library of Congress Cataloging-in-Publication Data

Britton, Tamara L., 1963-
    Devils Tower / Tamara L. Britton.
       p. cm. -- (Symbols, landmarks, and monuments)
    Includes bibliographical references and index.
    ISBN 1-59197-833-5
    1. Devils Tower National Monument (Wyo.)--Juvenile literature. I. Title.

F767.D47.B75 2005
978.7'13--dc22
                                                          2004050851

Contents

Devils Tower

Devils Tower is America's first national monument. It is in northeastern Wyoming on the banks of the Belle Fourche River. The national monument covers 1,347 acres (545 ha).

Native Americans were the first to call the area around Devils Tower home. To them, the land was sacred. So, they performed **rituals** and dances there.

As the nation became more populated, white settlers took the Native Americans' land. The native people were forced into small areas. Later, the Native Americans also lost these areas, including their land around the tower.

Devils Tower

Today, more than 450,000 people visit Devils Tower each year. Thousands of rock climbers have reached its summit. In June, Native Americans observe ancient **rituals** at the tower. America's first national monument is a symbol of the nation's desire to save the land for future generations.

As part of the national monument, the grounds around Devils Tower are protected against development.

Fast Facts

√ Colonel Richard Dodge is credited with giving the name *Devils Tower* to the rock formation in 1875. Dodge took the Native American name *The Bad God's Tower* and gave it the common name for the bad god.

√ According to Kiowa legend, one day some bears chased seven little girls. They ran from the bears and jumped upon a rock. There, one prayed to the rock, "Rock take pity on us, rock save us!" The rock heard their cries and began to grow. It pushed the girls up into the sky where they remain today. They are the seven stars that make up the Pleiades constellation.

√ The Battle of the Little Bighorn is also called "Custer's Last Stand."

√ There is a large prairie dog town that lies between the base of the tower and the Belle Fourche River.

√ On August 19, 1994, six-year-old Eric Peterson became the youngest person to climb Devils Tower.

Timeline

1868   √   The U.S. government signed a treaty that gave the Black Hills area to the Native Americans.

1874   √   Gold was discovered in the Black Hills.

1876   √   Native Americans and the U.S. Army fought the Battle of the Little Bighorn.

1891   √   The Forest Reserve Act was passed on March 31.

1893   √   William Rogers and Willard Ripley became the first people to climb the tower using a ladder they had built.

1906   √   The Antiquities Act of 1906 was passed; President Theodore Roosevelt named Devils Tower the first national monument on September 24.

1916   √   The National Park Service was started.

1917   √   The first road was built to the tower.

1928   √   A bridge was built over the Belle Fourche River.

1937   √   The first climb using rock-climbing techniques was done.

1938   √   A museum was built at Devils Tower.

Geology

From the open prairie of eastern Wyoming rises a column of rock. It towers over the banks of the Belle Fourche River. There are many theories concerning the origin of Devils Tower.

One theory states that the tower began forming about 60 million years ago. This happened when **molten** rock forced its way upward into the earth's crust. However, the rock stopped just below the earth's surface.

Eventually, the lava cooled into very hard rock called phonolite porphyry (FOH-nuh-lite POHR-fuh-ree). This hard column of rock remained buried in the surrounding soil. As time passed, the soft earth around the column began to **erode**. Soon, the pillar of rock was exposed.

Today, the column stands 1,267 feet (386 m) above the river. Its flat top is 5,117 feet (1,560 m) above sea level. But, the soil surrounding the tower continues to slowly erode. So as time passes, more of Devils Tower will be exposed.

Though Devils Tower appears to be just a large rock, many plants and animals call it home. Birds and chipmunks live on the top. Grasses, prickly pear cacti, **lichens**, sage, and mosses live on the tower, too.

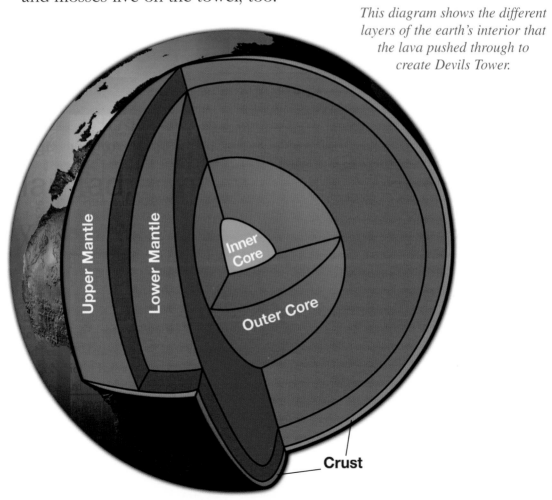

This diagram shows the different layers of the earth's interior that the lava pushed through to create Devils Tower.

Upper Mantle

Lower Mantle

Inner Core

Outer Core

Crust

Native Americans

The first people to call Devils Tower home were Native Americans. Sioux, Cheyenne, Arapaho, Crow, Shoshone, and Kiowa peoples lived there.

The Native Americans had different names for the tower. Some called it The Bad God's Tower. Early maps of the region have the tower's name as *Mato Tepee*. This means "Grizzly Bear Lodge."

There are many Native American legends that explain how the tower came to be. In the Cheyenne legend, a bear captured a woman and took her back to his cave. Her husband and his six brothers went to save her.

The youngest brother had great power. He dug into the bear's den and helped the woman escape. The woman and the brothers ran from the bear and his followers.

Shoshone children dance in traditional Native American dress.

Native Americans believe that these ridges were created by a bear trying to reach the top.

The youngest brother took a small rock and began to sing. When he finished singing, the rock had grown to the size of today's tower.

From the top, the brothers killed the bear's followers. They also killed the leader. But, only after he had clawed the tower trying to get at them. That is how the ridges on the tower's sides came to be.

Because of its magic, the tower was a sacred place to Native Americans. They held ceremonies and observed **rituals** at the base. These rituals included sweat lodge ceremonies, vision quests, and the sun dance.

Native American Rituals

Many Native American rituals are performed at Devils Tower. These rituals include sweat lodge ceremonies and vision quests.

During a sweat lodge ceremony, a hut, lodge, or cavern is heated by steam from water poured on hot stones. This is the traditional way of cleansing the body, mind, and spirit through ritual sweating and prayer.

A vision quest is a solitary watch by an adolescent Native American boy. His quest is to seek spiritual power and learn through a vision the identity of his guardian spirit. This spirit is usually an animal or a bird.

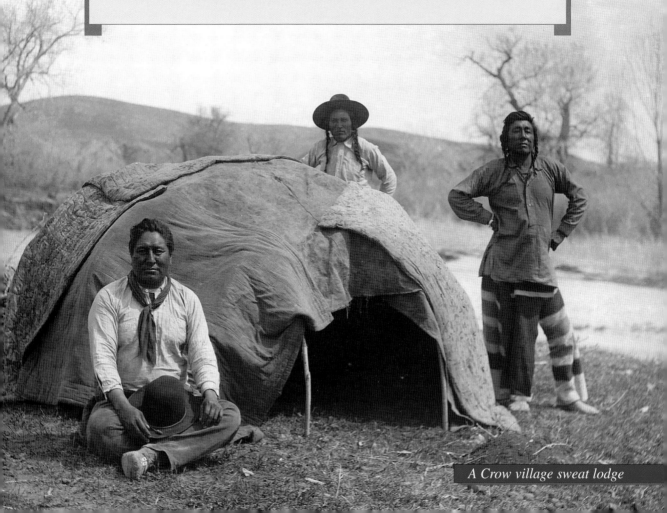

A Crow village sweat lodge

White Settlement

In 1776, the United States was founded. White settlers rushed to the new country. Soon, eastern lands were crowded. Settlers began to move west.

As the nation expanded, settlers claimed land that belonged to Native Americans. For years, Native Americans had lived happily near the tower and in the nearby Black Hills. So in 1868, the U.S. government signed the Treaty of Fort Laramie that gave the Sioux this area.

Then in 1874, gold was discovered in the Black Hills. The white settlers wanted the gold. So, the U.S. government tried to buy the land. They also tried to force the Native Americans onto **reservations**. But, the Native Americans did not want to sell their sacred land.

Devils Tower rises out of the Black Hills in northeastern Wyoming. Because of the discovery of gold, nearby towns such as Deadwood, South Dakota, sprang up overnight.

By 1876, the Native Americans feared losing all their land in the Black Hills region. They continued fighting the U.S. Army to maintain control of their land.

In June of that year, the U.S. Army fought Sioux and Cheyenne at the Battle of the Little Bighorn. During the battle, the Native Americans killed Lieutenant Colonel George Armstrong Custer and all his troops.

The defeat of the U.S. Army angered many Americans. So, the government sent in troops to invade the Native American lands.

The U.S. Army and the Native Americans continued to fight bitterly. But, the native people were outnumbered and had fewer weapons. By the fall of 1876, they were forced to **cede** the Black Hills and much of Wyoming to the U.S. government.

Opposite page: *Custer's last words are said to have been, "Hurrah, boys, we've got them! We'll finish them up and then go home to our station."*

George Armstrong Custer was born on December 5, 1839, in New Rumley, Ohio. In 1861, Custer graduated last in his class from the U.S. Military Academy at West Point. After graduation, he served in the Civil War. Custer was known for being stubborn and hotheaded. He was court-martialed in 1867. And, he was then suspended for one year for leaving an assignment. On June 25, 1876, Lieutenant Colonel Custer led an attack on Native Americans living in the Black Hills of South Dakota. This battle led to Custer's death.

National Monument

The U.S. government had finally acquired the land that included Devils Tower. But, many people did not want the tower to be owned by one person who would **exploit** it for profit. So, they worked to keep Devils Tower and its surrounding land free from settlement.

In August 1890, the General Land Office issued an order to reject any claims for these lands. It passed the Forest Reserve Act of March 31, 1891, to make sure the order was followed.

But, officials knew they needed to do more to save the tower. Wyoming's senator Francis E. Warren sponsored a bill to make Devils Tower a national park. Warren introduced the bill in July 1892, but it did not pass.

Then, the Antiquities Act of 1906 was passed. It authorized the president to issue **proclamations** that would set aside objects of historic or scientific interest.

These objects would become national monuments, which would be preserved for future generations. Under the Antiquities Act, President Theodore Roosevelt named Devils Tower the first national monument on September 24, 1906.

President Roosevelt

Devils Tower Proclamation

September 24, 1906.

BY THE PRESIDENT OF THE UNITED STATES OF AMERICA.

A PROCLAMATION.

Devils Tower National Monument, Wyo.
Preamble.
Ante, p. 225.

Whereas, It is provided by section two of the Act of Congress, approved June 8, 1906, entitled, "An Act for the preservation of American Antiquities," "That the President of the United States is hereby authorized, in his discretion, to declare by public proclamation historic land marks, historic and prehistoric structures, and other objects of historic or scientific interest that are situated upon the lands owned or controlled by the Government of the United States to be National Monuments, and may reserve as a part thereof parcels of land, the limits of which in all cases shall be confined to the smallest area compatible with the proper care and management of the object to be protected;"

And, whereas, the lofty and isolated rock in the State of Wyoming, known as the "Devils Tower," situated upon the public lands owned and controlled by the United States is such an extraordinary example of the effect of erosion in the higher mountains as to be a natural wonder and an object of historic and great scientific interest and it appears that the public good would be promoted by reserving this tower as a National monument with as much land as may be necessary for the proper protection thereof;

National monument, Wyoming.

Now, therefore, I, THEODORE ROOSEVELT, President of the United States of America, by virtue of the power in me vested by section two of the aforesaid Act of Congress, do hereby set aside as the Devils Tower National Monument, the lofty and isolated rock situated in Crook County, Wyoming, more particularly located and described as follows, towit:

19

Tourist Attraction

Early visitors to the monument had a difficult time getting there. There were only rough roads and trails to the tower. Travelers from the east had to cross the Belle Fourche River. But, there was no bridge. So, if the river's water level rose during their visit, they had to wait for it to go down before they could leave.

In 1916, the National Park Service was created. It took control of the Devils Tower National Monument. The next year, the park service built the first road to the tower. A log shelter was built for visitors six years later. And in 1928, a bridge was finally built over the river.

More people visited the tower every year. New highways linked towns in the area and gave more people a way to get to the monument. The popularity of the automobile also increased the need for visitor facilities.

Over the years, many tourists have bought postcards of Devils Tower, such as this one from 1890.

3577a J. C. H. GRABILL, Official Photographer of the Black Hills & F. P. R. R., and Home Stake Mining Co. Studios: Deadwood and Lead City, South Dakota.

In the 1930s, the nation was gripped by the **Great Depression**. However, it was during these trying times that much happened at the monument.

In 1933, President Franklin D. Roosevelt created the Civilian Conservation Corps (CCC). The CCC was meant to relieve **unemployment**. This program gave young people jobs completing public works projects. In 1935, a CCC camp was built at Devils Tower.

For the next three years, the men built new roads and footpaths. They created picnic areas with tables. Campgrounds for tents and trailers were constructed, too. And, plumbing and electrical systems were installed.

Because of these improvements, the number of visitors to the monument climbed steadily. Then, a museum was built in 1938. By 1941, almost 33,000 people a year came to see Devils Tower.

Opposite page: *A map of Devils Tower National Monument. Wyoming is home to both the first national monument and the first national park, Yellowstone National Park.*

DEVILS TOWER
NATIONAL MONUMENT

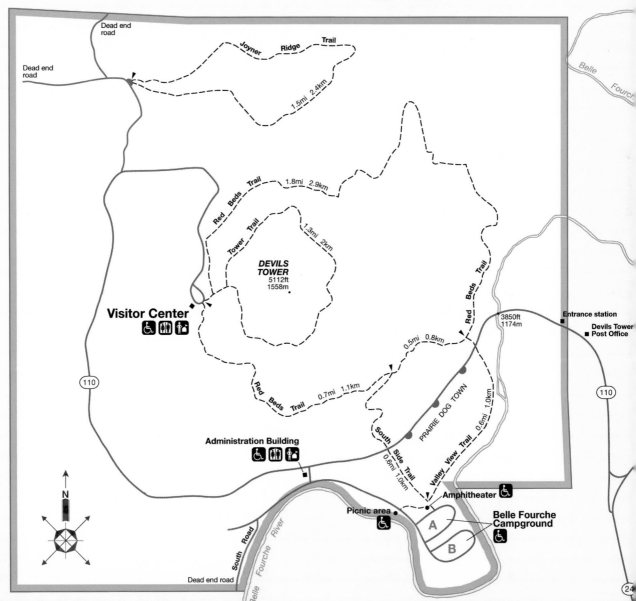

Hiking trail
Unpaved road
Parking area or turnout
0.3mi / 0.5km Distance indicator

Ranger station
Wheelchair accessible
Restrooms

Dead end road

Dead end road

Joyner Ridge Trail

1.5mi 2.4km

Red Beds Trail

1.8mi 2.9km

Tower Trail

1.3mi 2km

DEVILS TOWER
5112ft
1558m

Red Beds Trail

Visitor Center

3850ft
1174m

Entrance station

Devils Tower
Post Office

110

0.5mi 0.8km

Red Beds Trail 0.7mi 1.1km

PRAIRIE DOG TOWN

110

Administration Building

South Side Trail
0.6mi 1.0km

Valley View Trail 0.6mi 1.0km

N

Amphitheater

Picnic area

Belle Fourche Campground

A

B

South Road

Belle Fourche River

Dead end road

Belle Fourche

The Tower Conquered

Most early visitors to Devils Tower enjoyed its beauty from the ground. But, many people wondered what it would be like to stand on top of the tower. It wasn't long before someone found out!

In 1893, William Rogers and Willard Ripley built a ladder up the tower. They hammered pegs into parallel cracks in the rock and joined each set of pegs with a wooden step. Rogers and Ripley were the first people ever to see the view from the tower's summit.

Two years later, Rogers's wife Linnie became the first woman to reach the top. In 1937, members of the American **Alpine** Club of New York City climbed the tower using rock-climbing methods. Several years later, 16 members of the Iowa Mountain Climbers Club reached the summit and spent the night.

Many alpine clubs send members up Devils Tower.

Soon, someone decided to get to the top from the air instead of the ground! On October 1, 1941, George Hopkins **parachuted** from a plane and landed on the tower. The plane also dropped a rope for him to use to **descend**. But, the rope landed on the side of the tower. So, Hopkins was stuck.

The park service had not given Hopkins permission for the stunt. However, park rangers tried to figure out how to get him down. Goodyear offered a blimp, and the U.S. Navy offered a helicopter for the rescue.

Finally on October 3, rangers called Jack Durrance who had climbed the tower in 1938. On October 6, Durrance and seven other climbers reached the top where Hopkins was waiting. They all made the rescue descent with few problems.

Climbing records at the tower have been kept since 1937. More than 80 routes have been established. Devils Tower can be climbed in all seasons.

Durrance is the easiest route to climb. There are tougher routes such as Assembly Line, One-Way Sunset, and Hollywood & Vine. Climbers of all levels can find a route up the tower.

Today, the ladder that Rogers and Ripley used is mostly destroyed. However, people use other methods to climb the tower. A campground is also available for visitors to take advantage of. Devils Tower continues to be a popular tourist destination.

The Tower Today

Two prairie dogs keep watch for intruders.

Today, more than 450,000 people visit Devils Tower each year. They hike, camp, and picnic in the surrounding area. Many enjoy watching the area's abundant wildlife.

Since the late 1930s, the tower has been a top destination for rock climbers. More than 4,000 people climb the tower each year. However, visitors are asked not to climb the tower in June.

The month of June is reserved for Native American **rituals**. The tower continues to be a sacred site for Native Americans. Vision quests and sweat lodge ceremonies are still practiced at the tower. Since 1983, the modern sun dance has been held there, too. It is a celebration of the beginning of summer.

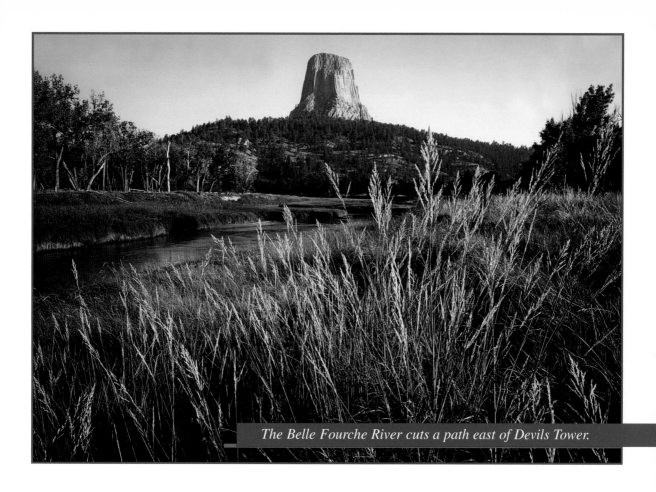

The Belle Fourche River cuts a path east of Devils Tower.

Devils Tower is the United States's first national monument. It is a symbol of the nation's commitment to maintaining its natural resources for generations of Americans.

Glossary

alpine - of or relating to mountains.

cede - to surrender possession of, typically by treaty.

descend - to move from a higher place to a lower one.

erode - to wash or wear away.

exploit - to use unfairly for selfish gain.

Great Depression - a period (from 1929 to 1942) of worldwide economic trouble when there was little buying or selling, and many people could not find work.

lichen - a mosslike plant.

molten - melted by heat.

parachute - a device consisting of a large sheet from which a person or object hangs. A parachute is used to slow a fall after jumping from an aircraft.

proclamation - an official public announcement.

reservation - a piece of land set aside by the government for Native Americans to live on.

ritual - a form or order to a ceremony.

unemployment - the state of being without a job.

Web Sites

To learn more about Devils Tower, visit ABDO Publishing Company on the World Wide Web at **www.abdopub.com**. Web sites about Devils Tower are featured on our Book Links page. These links are routinely monitored and updated to provide the most current information available.

Index